How Prints Look

HOW PRINTS LOOK

Photographs with a Commentary

BY

W. M. IVINS, Jr.

Remember that there are parts of what it most concerns you
to know which I cannot describe to you; you must come with
me and see for yourselves. The vision is for him who will
see it.   *Plotinus*

BEACON PRESS   BOSTON

The text of this volume is a photographic reproduction of that in the first edition, which was published by the Metropolitan Museum of Art, in New York, in 1943. As the original negatives and photographs for eleven of the illustrations have been lost, new ones have had to be made to take their places.

In the first edition the writer expressed his thanks to the late Alice Newlin and to Jean Leonard, Roberta Fansler (now Mrs. John Alford), and A. Hyatt Mayor for their most valuable criticism of the text. The excellent photographs on pages 4, 7, 8, 9, 10, 11, 16, 24, 25, 36, 74, 101, 102, 134, and 135 of this reprint were made by the photographers of the Metropolitan Museum of Art. The others were made by the writer from his 35-millimeter negatives.

W.M.I. Jr.

Woodbury, Conn.
August 1957

William M. Ivins, Jr. was the Curator of Prints at the Metropolitan Museum of Art in New York from 1916 to his retirement in 1946. He is the author of many articles and some books, including *Art and Geometry* and *Prints and Visual Communication*.

INTRODUCTORY NOTES

This book is an elementary introduction to the appearances (the outward and visible signs) of prints. It is not a history, and it contains no technical recipes or instructions for print making. Most of the time spent over it should be given to looking at its pictures.

The legends under the illustrations are integral parts of the text. The names of the artists and of the prints reproduced are given in the Table of Illustrations.

The illustrations nearly all reproduce details of prints. With few exceptions they have been enlarged, some of them very considerably. This has been done because the specific qualities of line and surface produced by the various graphic processes frequently lie below the threshold of unpracticed vision. No notation has been made of the scales of magnification, which vary according to the characteristics which it was desired to illustrate.

Just as on the street it is often impossible to recognize a still figure a long way off but easy to do so the moment it begins to move, so with practice in looking it will be discovered that the lines produced by each graphic process have a characteristic gait or motion of progress that is frequently recognizable even when the lines are too small to be seen clearly or singly. On occasion, however, the diagnosis of process becomes exceedingly difficult, and no one can be expected to make no mistakes. In spite of much care that has been taken there are undoubtedly such mistakes in this book.

Eighteenth-century woodcutter's knives, showing how the blade is inserted in a cleft handle, which is then bound with cord to hold the blade tight.

The method of cutting a wood block as practiced in the eighteenth century. At the top a small block is laid on a book so that it may be the more easily turned while being cut. In the middle the woodcutter makes a cut along the side of each of a series of parallel lines. At the bottom he makes the second cut needed to disengage the sliver of wood along the side of the line.

5

Seventeenth-century burins, or gravers, showing the whole tool, the cutting point, and the method of sharpening it.

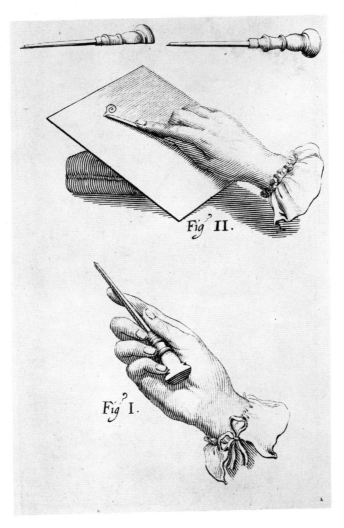

Fig. II.

Fig. I.

Seventeenth-century burins, or gravers, showing the way in which they were held and used on copper plates. The plates were balanced on little pads so that they could the more easily be turned for convenience in working. The plate was pushed against the tool just as much as the tool was pushed against the plate.

An eighteenth-century illustration of two mezzotint rockers, one big, for laying the original ground, and one small, for retouching, together with a combination tool having a three-cornered knife at one end and a burnisher at the other, with which to cut away and burnish down the mezzotint ground or burr. The shaded lines (a, b, in A) represent lines deeply engraved on the surface (c in B). When the tool is ground to a bevel (d in B) these lines make very fine teeth along the curved bottom of the tool. The rocker is held upright and pushed while being rocked back and forth with its rounded edge pressing on the plate. The illustration on this page represents other eighteenth-century tools. An etching needle with one point, and others with several points for use in stippling. A graver with two points to make two lines at once. Round-headed tools and roulette wheels with patterns of jagged points on their heads and circumferences. Specimens of the textures produced by these tools.

9

A seventeenth-century etching or engraving press, showing how the bed of the press, on which were laid the inked plate, the dampened paper, and a pile of felts or blankets, was pulled between two rollers.

A nineteenth-century wood engraver's hands, showing how he held his block balanced on a pad and how he held his engraving tool as he pushed the block against it.

FIRST PRINCIPLES

If a drawing is made with a greasy pigment (*e.g.* printer's ink, oil paint, lipstick, etc.) upon a smooth nonabsorbent surface and a piece of soft paper is then pressed down upon it the pigment will leave the smooth surface and adhere to the paper. The pressure can be applied in various ways, as by rubbing the back of the paper, or, if the surface be a sheet of metal, by running the surface and the paper through a clothes wringer or an etching press. Prints made in this way are called monotypes because only one good impression of each can be made.

The difficulty of remaking or renewing identically the same greasy drawing upon the smooth surface, once an impression has been taken from it, is so great that for practical purposes it is impossible unless the surface has been treated in some way so that this renewal can be done mechanically and not by redrawing. These methods of treatment of the printing surfaces and the ways of printing from them are called the graphic processes or techniques. In the beginning of their use the graphic techniques were comparatively simple. As time has gone by they have greatly increased in number and in technical complexity. It must be remembered that command over technical complexity, while requiring patience and skill, has little or no relation to creative artistry. One of the main reasons that so many artistically successful woodcuts, etchings, and lithographs have been made is the basic simplicity of those processes.

There are three great general groups or families of processes for treating a surface so that greasy ink may be mechanically deposited upon it in a predetermined and unvarying pattern. These families are known respectively as the planographic, relief, and intaglio processes. Each requires its own special kinds of tools, presses, inks, and incidental methods and materials, though many of these can be used interchangeably in producing either relief or intaglio printing surfaces.

In the following pages no attempt is made to do more than to describe the general principles underlying the great historic processes. For more detailed information, recipes, instructions, special tools, and materials, reference may be had to any number of technical treatises.

This is a slightly reduced reproduction of a monotype drawn on a polished metal plate with oil paint and a brush, and printed in an etching press before the paint dried. The reproduction shows the typical texture of the Chinese paper upon which the monotype was printed. Only one good impression of a monotype can be printed, but if, before an impression has dried, a piece of paper is laid upon its surface and the two are passed through a press, another, but paler, impression (a counterproof), in the opposite direction, can be obtained.

THE PLANOGRAPHIC OR LITHOGRAPHIC
PROCESSES

Lithography was invented just before 1800 by Alois Senefelder, a Bavarian.

The texture of a lithographic stone is such that when water is poured or wiped over its clear surface, it will hold the water all over in a thin film. If the surface is greasy in any place, however, no water will remain there. When a roller charged with greasy ink is passed over such a moistened surface, the ink will leave the roller and adhere to the greasy spots on the surface but will not adhere to the wet spots. Up to a certain point the more grease there is on any spot the more ink will be left there by the roller. Certain other materials share this peculiar quality of the lithographic stone, e.g., zinc that has been given a specially granulated surface. If a piece of paper, properly dampened, is laid upon the inked stone and rubbed down on it the ink will leave the stone and adhere to the paper, but the original grease marks will be left on the stone so that the process of dampening its surface, inking, and printing may be repeated without having to make the greasy marks again.

The various developments of these simple facts are too complicated and ingenious to be gone into here. There is an infinite number of ways of making the greasy marks on the stone—with a pen or brush loaded with thin grease in the form of an ink ("tusche") or with solid grease of different degrees of hardness put up in the form of crayons or pencils. The crayons and ink are made black so that their marks on the stone can be seen by the artist while he is making his drawing. Even the invisible, faint grease mark left on a stone by a sweaty finger will print. The grain of the stone surface, as it is finer or coarser, plays its part in the quality of the lines made upon it.

Lithographs are printed in a press specially designed to rub the back of the paper as it lies on the inked stone. The stone lies on a traveling bed that moves on rollers. After it is inked the dampened paper is laid upon it. On top of that a piece of thin, shiny cardboard is laid. The bed with its burden is then passed under a round edge which squeezes the cardboard and paper against the stone. When all the prints that are needed have been printed, the stone can be resurfaced, by grinding it down, and then used for another lithograph. In this way many stones have been in constant use for many years. The stones are thick, heavy, and clumsy.

This is an approximately natural-size detail from a lithograph in which much work was done with a crayon and by scraping and scratching. Some of the smooches look as though they may have been made with the artist's forefinger or with a rag.

This is a detail from a pen lithograph. The artist made his drawing on the stone with a soft quill pen and a thin, greasy liquid ink.

This is a detail from a wash lithograph. The artist worked on the stone with a water-color brush and thin ink, just as though he were making a wash drawing on a piece of paper. The typical "hard edges" of water color are visible.

This is a detail from a scratch lithograph. The artist covered a dry stone with lithographic ink or thick heavy crayon and then scratched out his lights with a point. The white lines have the crumbly, broken character of scratches on polished stone—which is what they actually are.

A drawing made on paper with a lithographic crayon can be transferred to the stone by laying the drawing face down on the stone and passing it through the press. While this can be done with almost any kind of paper it is usually done with specially prepared "transfer paper." Some transfer papers are transparent so that they can be used to make tracings with. Thus it is possible for the artist to make his drawings anywhere that he can work on paper without having to carry the heavy stones about with him or having laboriously to copy his drawings onto a stone. Many of Whistler's lithographs were drawn on paper. The sitter for one of Whistler's lithographic portraits told the present writer that he redid his drawing almost forty times, working on transparent transfer papers laid down one on top of another so that he could use his last drawing as a tracing guide for his next one.

Naturally the texture of the transfer paper shows in transfer lithographs. Additional textures can be got by placing the transfer paper on a book cover, a textile, and so forth, while it is being drawn upon. Some painters, e.g., Fantin-Latour, have made their drawings for paintings on transfer paper and when one has proved specially attractive have had it transferred to the stone, worked it up, and then published it as a lithograph. It is not necessary that the artist who "makes a lithograph" should know anything about the technique of lithography, or even have seen either a stone or a press. The artist can make a drawing in lithographic crayon on paper and let the printer do the rest. Joseph Pennell, Whistler's friend and biographer, told the writer that Whistler was almost completely ignorant of the technique of lithography.

A fresh print from a stone can be laid face down on another stone and run through the press, thus transferring the drawing to the second stone. In this way it is possible to print editions of the same lithograph from two or more different stones and so save time in production. Similarly, fresh prints from etched or engraved plates can be transferred to stone and then printed as lithographs. Sheet music used to be made this way.

This is a detail from a transfer lithograph. The paper, while it was being drawn upon, was probably laid upon a pebbled cloth book cover or portfolio.

This is a detail from a newspaper caricature which started as a lithographic drawing on a stone. A print from the stone was transferred to a metal plate, which was then etched so that the whites were lower than the blacks. The plate was then printed, as though it were a woodcut, in the same press and at the same time as the text of the newspaper in which the caricature appeared. The impression of the lines into the paper can be seen in the reproduction.

THE RELIEF PROCESSES

WOODCUTS

The oldest of the relief processes is the woodcut. It was used for printing textiles more than a thousand years ago, and in Europe it began to be used for the printing of pictures some time about 1400 A.D.

The woodcutter, with small knives and gouges, cuts away the wood from between the lines that he or a draughtsman has drawn on the smooth surface of a piece of wood. When carefully done the process can produce a fairly good reproduction of a pen line. Each side of the line has to be cut separately. Thus where the etcher or engraver thinks of a line as the trace of a single gesture, the woodcutter has to think of each single line as the result of several separate gestures.

The kinds of knives and gouges used depend upon personal preference and to some extent upon the fineness of the work to be done. Excellent work has been done with ordinary pen knives and scalpels. The illustrations on pages 4 and 5 show the knives used by the French woodcutter Papillon in the eighteenth century. The finer the grain of the wood and the higher the polish it will take, the finer the work that can be done on it. Apple, pear, box, and even maple are used. Woodcuts are usually made on the sides of blocks cut plankwise from the tree ("side wood"), though they are sometimes made on blocks that are cut in cross section from the tree ("end wood").

A block can be printed by rubbing the back of a piece of paper laid face down on its inked surface. Many of the early fifteenth-century woodcuts were printed by rubbing, as were some of the "block books," *i.e.*, books the texts and pictures of which were cut on wood blocks. The lines on the back of a rubbed woodcut are usually shiny. Since the second half of the fifteenth century woodcuts have customarily been printed in ordinary type printing presses, and—for convenience in printing with and at the same time as type—their thickness is usually the height of the type ("type high"). Until the introduction of very smooth papers in quite modern times, the paper was always printed upon in a moist condition. Prior to the nineteenth century both type and blocks were inked by pounding them with stuffed leather "balls" on which the ink had been evenly spread. This method of inking put ink on the sides of the upstanding lines on the wood block as well as on their tops. Between 1810 and 1820 ink rollers came into use—at first in England.

This is a reproduction, approximately natural size, of a portion of a late fifteenth-century German wood block from which a great number of impressions has been printed. The tops of some of the lines were deliberately made lower in some places than in others, so as to increase or decrease the pressure of the press in particular places.

This is a reproduction, approximately natural size, of a portion of an impression presumably printed in the 1490's from the block reproduced on the opposite page.

This is a reproduction, approximately natural size, of a portion of an original sixteenth-century Flemish wood block, on which the artist had made his pen drawing and on which the cutter had begun his work. The cutting was never finished and the block was never printed.

26

This great enlargement shows a fifteenth-century Italian woodcut illustration running over the letter q in a text. Because of this we can tell that it was printed later than the text. It is in a thinner ink than the text. It was not printed by rubbing, and it probably was printed not in a press but by pressing the inked block on the paper by hand, somewhat as if it were a rubber stamp. The impression from the wood block is light and uneven.

Educant oculi tui fidelis anima fletur
us compaßionis igne.considerans qu

This fifteenth-century Italian woodcut illustration was printed at the same time, in the same ink, in the same press as the type. First used in a book in 1467, but possibly made well before that time, it is one of the earliest reproductions of a picture.

A very few early woodcuts were conceived in terms of knife work rather than in terms of pen drawing. This is Italian fifteenth-century work.

This is a detail from an impression of an early sixteenth-century German wood block in which the woodcutter cut out the artist's lines instead of the spaces between them, so that they appear in the print as white lines on a black ground. This impression was printed from a worm-eaten block. Two of the wormholes printed white and someone drew lines over them in pen and ink, as is clearly shown in the reproduction.

This is a detail from an impression of a fifteenth-century Italian wood
block the work upon which was carried out both in black lines on a
white ground and in white lines on a black ground. In the solid blacks
the hollows between the ribs of the paper show as uneven, paler streaks.
A solid black is one of the most difficult things to print evenly on handmade paper (compare p. 38).

Sometimes it is difficult to tell whether the lines in a print are black on a white ground or white on a black ground. This is Dutch work of the seventeenth century.

On rare occasion the artist and the woodcutter made stylistic capital of the fact that, while for the etcher or engraver a line is the result of one gesture of the hand, in cutting a block each of the two edges of a line has to be separately disengaged from the wood. This is eighteenth-century English work.

German woodcut designers habitually used the regular calligraphic drawing of their national school (see pages 25, 35, and 36), and in a formalized way. The Italians drew and cut on their blocks much more freely and naturally (see pages 29, 31, and 38). Here a sixteenth-century Italian drew on the block as freely as though sketching on paper.

This is an approximately natural-size reproduction of a fine impression of a sixteenth-century German woodcut in which the artist drew his lines very close together so as to produce an effect of tones. The cutter produced a very good "facsimile" of the artist's pen lines.

A

B

C

D

A is a "proof" impression of an early sixteenth-century German woodcut with exceptionally fine and minute lines. It has always been considered one of the greatest technical triumphs of woodcutting. B is an impression from the same block as it was printed in a mid-nineteenth-century book. C is a copy engraved, not cut, on wood before the invention of photography. It was considered a very remarkable performance. D is an original "proof" impression of another subject from the same series. All are reproduced in approximately their natural size.

This is a detail from D on the opposite page. Notice the shading in the cheek, which is hardly visible in the natural size. The way in which the tops of the lines printed paler than the blobbets of ink on the sides of the lines can be easily seen, as also how the ink clogged up the spaces between the fine lines (*e.g.*, in the eye).

This is a detail from a finely drawn and cut Italian sixteenth-century wood block printed upon paper the horizontal ribs in which were coarser than the lines of the block.

METAL CUTS

In the late 1400's men began to use relief printing surfaces of metal as well as of wood. On rare occasion it is difficult to tell at first glance whether a print was pulled from a metal or a wooden surface. There is no practical difference between the ways in which wood and metal relief surfaces receive and deposit ink. In making metal cuts the old engravers cut away from the surfaces of their metal plates the parts that were not to print, just as the woodcutters did with wood blocks, except that instead of using knives and gouges they used the punches and engraving tools used by silversmiths and goldsmiths for the decoration of their wares. The metal plates, after being engraved, were fastened on pieces of wood and then printed as though they were woodcuts. Some engraver's tools are reproduced on pages 6 and 7.

In the late 1790's William Blake, in making the relief metal plates for his *Songs of Innocence,* drew his designs on clean copper plates with a brush and liquid etching ground, and then etched away the whites. The so-called line and halftone cuts in our modern periodicals, books, and newspapers, are usually printed from etched relief metal plates made by photomechanical process.

This detail from a late fifteenth-century German metal cut shows that the metal plate was mounted on a piece of wood. The head of one of the nails that held the plates on the wood can be seen above the halo. The difference between the engraved lines and the punched dots and patterns is obvious.

This is a detail from an illustration in a lay prayer book printed on vellum at Paris in 1498. The original engraved relief plate of copper from which it was printed was recently in a private collection in Paris. The plate was used to print from as late as 1899. Compare the white flicks in the ground with the flicks in the illustrations on pages 56 and 95.

Blake, instead of engraving away the whites in his relief metal printing surfaces, etched them away. He claimed that the technique was revealed to him in a dream. It is now a standard part of all modern photomechanical relief processes. Blake printed these relief plates in single colors, *e.g.,* red or green, and afterwards painted them up with water colors more or less elaborately as he received more or less money for them.

This is a detail from a French nineteenth-century newspaper cartoon some of the lines in which look as though they had possibly been executed in a variety of the "chalk plate" technique. In this process a layer of chalk was spread over a flat metal plate. The artist then scratched his lines through the chalk down to the metal surface. The plate was then used as the mold for a casting in type metal. The type metal cast was then printed like a woodcut. Sometimes white lines were engraved in the broader blacks of the casting.

WOOD ENGRAVING

In 1722 at London there was issued Croxall's modest, badly printed edition of *Aesop's Fables* illustrated with little white-line relief cuts engraved on metal by William Kirkall. In the second half of the eighteenth century Thomas Bewick, a plate engraver of Newcastle upon Tyne, discovered that if he used a piece of end wood (see page 23) he could engrave upon it just as the makers of metal cuts and copper engravings had engraved upon their metal plates, provided he held his tool in a slightly different way (see pages 7 and 11). Except in "facsimile cuts" of pen drawings, the engraved lines in a wood engraving appear white on a black ground. Bewick and his pupils made many experiments in the new technique. Their discoveries soon became common practice in England and slowly spread to the continent of Europe and to America. By the middle of the nineteenth century the wood-engraving techniques were in universal use as the standard ways of illustrating books and magazines and remained as such until the end of the century, when photomechanical processes displaced them for all except some limited and usually self-conscious purposes.

The number of wood engravings reproduced here is perhaps larger than is necessary to show the bare process divorced from the drawing of the lines it was used to produce. By increasing the number it has been possible to show how the wood engravers' minds were so conditioned, as the psychologists say, by the other more familiar kinds of printed pictures, that they spent much of their time imitating other processes rather than in discovering the peculiar qualities and freedoms of their own. This is a trait common to all men using a new process. It is particularly noticeable in wood engraving, which is, except for lithography, the youngest of the classical graphic processes.

In the middle of the nineteenth century people began to print photographs upon blocks of end wood, which were then engraved. This eliminated the draughtsman and was therefore regarded as a great step in advance. The process in general produced only rather poor handmade substitutes for the not yet invented "halftone," but two generations of people grew up who only knew the great paintings through these prints. Their effect upon American aesthetic ideas was very great.

This is a detail from one of the metal cuts in the Croxall *Aesop* of 1722, which is supposed to have given Bewick the idea of engraving upon wood. Bewick discovered that although an engraving tool will not work on side wood it will work upon end wood.

This is one of Bewick's own engravings on wood. Careful looking will show that he thought in terms of his whites and not of his blacks. The texture of his blocks was so fine that when really good impressions were wanted it was necessary to print them on the ribless paper that came from China in the tea boxes.

EMORY, wafted by thy gentle g

Bewick's pupil Luke Clennell showed that finer reproductions of pen drawings could be made by wood engraving than by woodcutting. When one of these prints is enlarged, however, as here, it betrays the fact that it was engraved and not cut, *e.g.,* the lines in the hair are white and not black lines. This minuteness of workmanship determined the way of most of nineteenth-century book illustration and brought about the general use of very smooth papers in books.

William Harvey imitated the artificial linear systems of the reproductive engravers on copper. It took him several years to engrave this block. When it was finished there was no type-printing press strong enough to print it, although it was only 14¾ by 11⅜ inches in size. Some years later, when a strong enough press was found, the little pieces of wood of which the block was formed had shrunk apart, and the white lines left by the cracks had to be retouched by hand. Only a few proofs were pulled on China paper, the sole paper then available that was smooth enough.

By the 1840's wood engraving had become a technical trade carried on in highly organized shops by many anonymous workers. Many of the important artists of the time made line drawings on blocks to be engraved in these shops. In spite of the routine nature of the engraving many of the "woodcuts" thus turned out were masterpieces of design. In designing this woodcut Daumier introduced a caricature of himself as the figure blowing the flageolet.

Comparatively few of the men who have engraved on wood have made their own designs. Among the great exceptions was William Blake, who, though a professional engraver on copper, must be regarded as an inspired amateur in his work on the wood, on which he sketched as freely with his engraving tool as he did with pencil on paper.

50

In the middle 1850's photography had reached such a state of development that it was possible to print photographs on wood blocks, which
could then be engraved. This made for a much greater accuracy in reproduction of works of art in relief printing surfaces than had ever before
been possible. Thomas Bolton, who engraved this, may have been the
first to photograph his subject onto his block. Curiously, the lines in this
print are "black" and not "white."

In spite of the fact that they could photograph their drawings onto the blocks, artists continued to draw directly on the blocks. Many of them, instead of making line drawings, made wash drawings on the blocks, which were then "interpreted" or "translated" by the engravers. This detail from a wash drawing on an uncut block by Mary Halleck Foote shows the rings of growth and the radial lines of the tree from which the end-wood block was cut.

The engraver to whom the block reproduced on the opposite page was sent liked the drawing on it so much that he kept it and had it photographed on another block, which he engraved instead. This detail from a print from the block that was engraved shows how the engraver translated the artist's tones into lines and dots.

Out of the routine anonymity of the engraving shops in America a few
men emerged as virtuosi of white-line engraving and achieved personal
recognition as artists. One of the best known of these virtuoso engravers
was Henry Wolf, who took pride in the accuracy with which he rendered
the color values of the tones in paintings. It is interesting to compare the
linear scheme shown in this detail from Wolf's wood engraving after a
painting in The Metropolitan Museum of Art with the seventeenth-century copper engraving reproduced on page 75.

This is a reproduction of a photograph of the detail of the painting reproduced in the engraving shown on the opposite page.

Another, perhaps the most famous, virtuoso engraver was Timothy Cole, whose prints after paintings by the old masters were very well known. Like those of Wolf, his originals were photographed onto his blocks before he engraved them.

This is a reproduction of the same detail shown on the opposite page, except that here an electrotype of the block was printed as though it were an etching. It shows that the wood engraving was a sort of adaptation of an eighteenth-century intaglio technique (see page 105) in reverse, in relief, and on wood instead of copper. The dots, however, being made with an engraving tool, have much the same shape as those in flicked engravings on copper (see page 95).

Of all the virtuoso wood engravers W. J. Linton was perhaps the most brilliant and expressive in his use of the engraving tool, as well as the freest and least subject to any established routine of linear system.

THE INTAGLIO PROCESSES

Any slightest scratch or mark that disturbs the surface of a highly polished plate of metal will hold printer's ink and can be printed. It is possible to make pits, scratches, or incisions in the surface of a copper plate that are so fine and close together that prints from them appear as unbroken tints to the naked eye. Each such dot or line, no matter how small it is, has the specific character that accompanies the technical means by which it was made. Thus, for example, an etched line has the same character whether it be microscopically fine or so bold and coarse that it can be felt with the finger tip.

The three basic types of "intaglio" work upon metal (usually copper) plates are drypoint, engraving, and etching. All the other methods belong to one or several of these basic types.

In *drypoint* the surface of the plate is torn by a sharp round point thrust into the surface and dragged along through it. The tool is held like a pencil. It is usually a small bar of steel, though sometimes a diamond point is used. The metal displaced by the motion of the point is not detached from the plate but stands up above it in a burr (*i.e.*, a rough ridge of sharp points) on either side of the trench, or rut, ploughed in the surface by the moving point. The cross section of the rut is V-shaped. The amount of burr thrown up depends upon how hard the point is pressed into the surface and the angle at which it enters it. The burr wears away very rapidly in the course of printing.

In *engraving* V-shaped trenches are cut in the surface of the plate by a tool called a graver, or burin, which is pushed along the surface. The graver is a bar of steel with a V-shaped cross section and a sharpened end, which acts like a scoop or gouge and cuts out a shaving from the metal surface along which it travels. It has a handle usually of wood, though frequently it is merely an old cork, which rests against the ball of the hand while the metal shaft is held in the fingers (see pages 6 and 7). No matter how sharp the graver is, it always leaves a minute burr along either side of the trench that it cuts in the metal surface. The early engravers let this burr wear away in the course of the printing of the plate. Later engravers scraped the burr away before they began to print their plates.

Etching is a process by which lines are eroded in the surface of a metal plate. The polished plate is covered with a specially prepared "ground," the principal component of which is wax. The grounded plate is then

59

blackened with smoke. The artist draws his design on the blackened ground with a point, or "etching needle." The size, shape, and weight of the tool are matters of personal convenience. Many etchers use sewing needles mounted in the ends of sticks of wood, others small sharpened bars of steel. Rops is said to have etched with a toothpick, and Turner with a fork that had lost all but one of its tines. In theory the etcher presses just hard enough on his point to scratch through the ground but not to dig into the plate. The lines then appear as bright metal against the blackened ground. Acid (frequently dilute nitric) is then applied to the grounded surface. It "bites," or dissolves away, the bright metal exposed in the lines, but does not go through the ground. The breadth of the lines depends to some extent upon the coarseness of the point, but usually more upon the length of time the lines are exposed to the acid. The depth of the lines depends entirely upon how long they are exposed to the acid. When a group of lines has been bitten enough, the acid is removed from the plate and a brush loaded with ground dissolved in a solvent is passed over them. The plate can then be returned to the acid for further biting of the lines not so "stopped out."

The three basic processes are frequently used in conjunction. An etched plate can be touched up or finished in either or both engraving and drypoint. Very fine engraving can be touched up in drypoint and the burr then removed from the drypoint touches. It is very difficult to distinguish between light engraved lines and drypoint lines from which the burr has been removed.

The vocabulary of the collectors and dealers is frequently very misleading and at variance with the actual technical facts. Many "etchings" contain much drypoint or engraving, and many "engravings" are almost entirely etching. Seymour Haden insisted that Meryon was not an etcher ("eau-fortiste") but a painter engraver ("peintre graveur") because he made so much use of the engraving tool in finishing his plates. From a strictly technical point of view the manner in which the lines in a print are laid has nothing to do with its classification as an etching or an engraving. Psychologically and practically, however, every intaglio print in which the lines are laid in a formal manner is an "engraving," and every one in which they are laid freely is an "etching." (Compare remarks on page 148.) Abraham Bosse, who wrote the first treatise on etching, used special etching needles that enabled him to make etched lines that looked like engraved lines. For reproductions of his work see pages 6, 7, 10.

The *method of printing intaglio plates* is basically the same no matter what particular processes have been used on them. Stiff, tacky ink is spread over the warm plate and worked down into its lines. The plate is then wiped with rags and finally with the palm of the hand to remove the ink from the metal surface but not from the lines or scratches in it. This done, the inked plate is laid face up upon the bed, or plank, of a roller (or etching) press. Damp paper is laid on the plate and over the paper are placed felts or pieces of blanket. The handles of the press are then pulled and the bed with its burden is run between two heavy rollers (see page 10). The pressure of the rollers on the blankets crushes the damp soft paper into the lines in the plate so that it takes up the ink from them.

Engravings are usually wiped "dry" so that no ink is left on the surface of the plate, but many etchers deliberately leave films of ink on the surfaces of their plates. Rembrandt and, especially, Whistler made much use of this trick, which became so popular at one time that Béraldi humorously complained that whereas in his youth etchings were made with a point and acid they were now made with a rag. The drier the plate the more brilliant is the contrast between the white of the paper and the black of the ink. There are many tricks of printing. A heavy-handed printer can wear out a plate very quickly, especially if it contains any drypoint. The burr on a drypoint or engraving catches and holds drifts of ink on its side just as a furrow holds drifts of snow on the side away from the rut. The strength and lasting power of the burr depend very largely upon the hardness of the copper plate. Modern rolled plates are not as hard as the old ones that were planished with a hammer on an anvil until they rang. As the burr wears away it holds less and less ink along its side. Thus what in an early impression may be a broad, juicy, blurry line, in a late impression may be a very hard, thin, dry one.

A copper plate can be "steel-faced" by electroplating it with a microscopically thin film of pure iron. The process is said to have been invented in Paris in 1857. It makes plates wear much longer, especially when they have any drypoint work on them. Given equal care in printing, no one can tell the difference between impressions from the copper and from the steel facing. Some of Whistler's most famous prints were first published from plates that had been steel-faced. Haden made it a regular practice to steel-face his plates and thanks to it he was able to print successive editions from many of them over periods as long as thirty years.

The limitation of the number of prints from a plate to a small number such as thirty or forty is not predicated upon wear of the plate but upon the immediate commercial advantages of a quick and artificial rarity.

When a drypoint plate is inked and wiped, ink is left alongside the burr on the lines just as a drift of snow is left by the wind alongside a furrow. This produces warm, furry lines that are alike in no two impressions. The earlier the impression is the higher and stronger the burr was on the plate at the time it was printed and the blurrier and softer the lines are apt to be on the print. (Compare pages 64 and 65.)

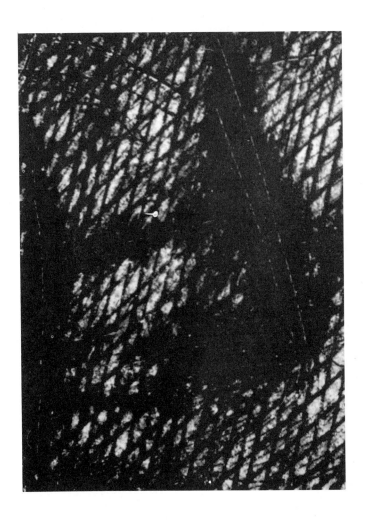

In very heavy drypoint the tops of the burr stick up through the ink on either side of it and sometimes in printing produce thin white lines like scratches in the heavy blacks.

The burr on drypoint lines, when not too heavy, can easily be burnished
down by rubbing with a piece of polished steel or an agate. Here it can
be seen how the artist changed his work on the plate (*e.g.,* in the left
eye) just as though he had been working with a pencil and an eraser on
paper.

This greatly enlarged detail from a very early impression of a late fifteenth-century German engraving shows how the engraver strengthened
several of a group of engraved lines by digging into them with a drypoint. The burr and the ink lying along it are very clearly visible.

Early impressions of many fifteenth-century Italian engravings have a
peculiarly soft, uneven quality of line quite unlike that with which we
are familiar in German prints.

Late impressions of such early Italian engravings have a hard, bare, stringy quality of line. Compare this late impression with the early one from the same plate on the opposite page.

In some very unusual early impressions of fifteenth-century Italian engravings the strong white lines of the burr can be seen. This enlargement makes these white lines easily visible.

This is a great magnification of several of the lines reproduced on the opposite page. The way the ink lies in the lee of the burr is plainly visible.

As the earlier engravers did not habitually scrape the burr from their lines the very early impressions from their plates are apt to have a peculiar warmth and fullness of line. This is a detail from a very rich early impression of a fifteenth-century German engraving.

On occasion there occur very pale impressions, almost without ink in their lines but printed from plates in perfect condition. These are some- times of great, though ghostly, beauty. They were presumably printed as a means of cleaning the plate after a day's printing. Nowadays plates are cleaned with benzine or gasoline.

The principal technical difference between early German and early Italian engraving is not so much in the printing quality of the lines as in the way they were drawn (or laid). The methods of laying lines on engraved plates corresponded closely with the methods of laying lines with pen and ink in use in each country. This detail is from an early sixteenth-century German print.

The German and Italian schools naturally influenced each other. Marc-antonio, a sixteenth-century Italian, in his later work produced a sort of synthesis of the linear schemes of the German woodcutters and the Italian copper engravers and started engraving on its way towards having its own specific methods of laying lines. The German print on the opposite page is a portrait of a surface, with all its little stresses and tautnesses. This Italian print is a schematic indication of the volumes that lie under a surface.

In the middle of the sixteenth century Dutch engravers began to make stylistic play with the capacity of the engraved line to start thin and sharp, swell to a certain thickness, and then taper away again.

In the seventeenth century in France a certain kind of lean stylization was carried very far. In the nineteenth century this was revived in some American white-line reproductive wood engraving (compare page 54).

Later the French developed a plumper but most methodical and artificial manner of laying lines, especially in "reproductive engravings" after paintings, drawings, sculpture, etc. To bring out its full brilliance it was necessary that the burr should be removed from the engraved lines before printing began.

Out of the precedents typified by the engraving on the preceding page there gradually evolved the "lozenge and dot" linear system familiar in "bank-note" engraving. This was possibly the most highly artificial convention ever adopted in the graphic arts. It had its origin in the economics of the business of making reproductive engravings (see page 147) but was long accepted by the public as the typical method of engraving.

How artificial the linear structure exemplified in the preceding illustration was, and how little needed for representation, is shown by this detail from a famous engraving by a mid-nineteenth-century French engraver, which is often pointed to as one of the great technical triumphs of engraving.

This is a detail from a modern impression from a flat piece of a twelfth-century chandelier that was decorated with engraved lines several hundred years before men learned how to print from engraved plates. Its artistic merit is as much greater than that of the prints reproduced in the preceding four or five illustrations as its technique is simpler and more rudimentary than theirs. It does not, however, begin to convey nearly as much information as they do about form and texture. The holes for the rivets that held the metal plate in place in the chandelier can be seen.

The details on this and on the opposite page illustrate the difference between typical engraved and etched lines. They are from two prints of the same size after the same painting. This is an engraving, the other is an etching. Both are seventeenth-century work.

As the etcher's point glides with perfect ease in all directions over the grounded plate, the lines made by it have a nervous, muscular tremor lacking in lines made by such tools as the drypoint and graver, which are pushed down into the metal and held stiffly by it. This slight tremor is perhaps the most easily recognizable characteristic of the etched line.

This greatly enlarged reproduction of a tiny figure from a dry-wiped impression of a seventeenth-century French etching on copper shows very clearly that etching is a process of erosion. The sides of the etched lines have the same character as the crumbling sides of a small rivulet in dry soil. The ends of the lines are blunt and not sharp as are the ends of engraved lines. Compare the quality of these lines with that of the engraved and drypoint lines reproduced on page 65.

The ease and quickness with which etching could be done made it a favorite medium not only for rapid sketches but for pictures with "news value." At a time when Lord Lovat, the last man to be beheaded in England, was much in the public eye, an artist made this rapid etched sketch of him and made a lot of money by selling prints at a shilling apiece.

The earliest etching plates were of iron. The earliest etchings on copper were made about 1520. In this print of that year both etching and engraving were used. As it was not practical to engrave on iron, this plate must have been of copper. With a little careful examination the two kinds of lines can be differentiated, *e.g.,* the coarse shading lines in the upper lip have blunt ends and are therefore etched.

Since about 1520 etching and engraving have been constantly used on the same plates. Some "etchings" have a very high proportion of engraving in them. This enlargement of a portion of the background in a famous nineteenth-century French etching shows that it was carried out in very delicate engraving from which the burr was not scraped away. Compare the quality of the lines with that of those reproduced on pages 66 and 68 above.

Details from two fine impressions of the same plate, which was first etched and then shaded and pointed up with engraving and drypoint. The left is the earlier impression. The right shows not only wear and the breakdown of lines but the introduction of new engraved lines to "pick up" the plate.

Etching has been used at various times to produce reproductions of paintings, drawings, etc. In these reproductive prints the etched line was frequently as artificial and stylized as that in any engraving. Prints like
this are called "engravings" but in fact they contain less engraving than
many "etchings."

Time was money in the routine engraving business as in some others. To speed up the work on a plate it was often carried as far as might be in etching and drypoint and finished in engraving. This explains why the first states of so many eighteenth-century engravings are referred to as the "etched states."

The reproduction on the opposite page shows the "etched state" (which includes much drypoint), and that on this page shows the finished state, of the same detail in a French eighteenth-century "engraving." The etching in work of this kind had naturally to be done in highly formalized lines of the same general character as the stylized engraved lines used in finishing.

Drypoint was frequently used with etching to gain added color and dramatic effect, as in this seventeenth-century Dutch print. The drag of the ink left on the surface of the plate in wiping it can be easily seen.

The heightening of the color and contrast obtainable by intentional manipulation of the ink during the process of wiping the plate began very early. This is a detail from a German etching on iron made in 1516, which was bitten so evenly all over that clean, evenly wiped impressions from it lacked contrast and sparkle and had a flat appearance. The finest early impressions from the plate were therefore deliberately wiped so as to leave more ink in the lines and on the surface of the plate in some places than in others.

This is a somewhat enlarged and greatly intensified reproduction specially made to emphasize the way in which a seventeenth-century Dutch artist left films of ink on certain parts of his plate. Although they are so slight as to be hardly visible in the original, they were very deliberately and carefully made and their artistic effect is very great.

A seventeenth-century Dutch artist, displeased with a passage in one of his prints, cut the surface of his plate away in that part, gave it a hasty burnishing, and reworked it in drypoint. The smooches were made by the ink held in the roughnesses that were left by the knife as it cut the surface away and that, through haste, were not burnished.

Shortly after 1500 some engravers found it desirable to make exactly repeatable smooches, tints, or tone shading. This detail from an early sixteenth-century Italian engraving shows one of the earliest attempts to solve the technical problem of producing tones that were definitely controlled through work on the plate. Here the engraver roughened the surface of his plate by rubbing it over with a fine abrasive, then burnished the parts he wanted to be brilliant, and finally engraved the lines on the plate.

This detail from another early sixteenth-century Italian engraving shows still another early method of producing tones, more laborious than that exemplified in the preceding illustration, but having the advantage that by its use soft lines as well as flat tones could be produced. This method consisted in dotting or flicking the copper with the point of the graver.

In the earliest years of etching men made experiments towards ways of producing more definitely controlled tones than was possible by mere skill in wiping their plates, and even of producing soft lines. It seems not to be definitely known how this early sixteenth-century German print was made, but it may well have been done in somewhat the manner exemplified in the next illustration.

In the seventeenth century Dutch etchers occasionally produced the minute dots or pits in the surfaces of their plates that were needed for a controlled tone effect by painting the plate with a mixture of oil and powdered sulphur, or some other chemical, which pitted the plate in a delicate tint. In this portrait important parts of the modeling are carried out in such a sulphur tint. Careful looking will discern burnisher marks and supplemental drypoint in the right eye and just under it, as well as in other places.

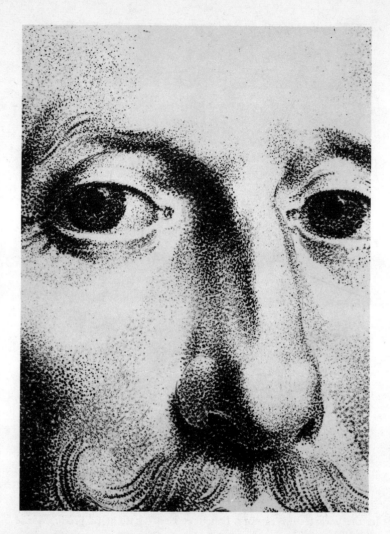

In the 1600's men began to experiment towards producing controlled tones on copper plates without the use of etching or the engraving tool. In this portrait practically all the work was done by hammering or tapping sharp points into the copper.

Some seventeenth-century Dutch experiments in tone look almost as though their effect had been achieved by rolling rattail files over etched plates.

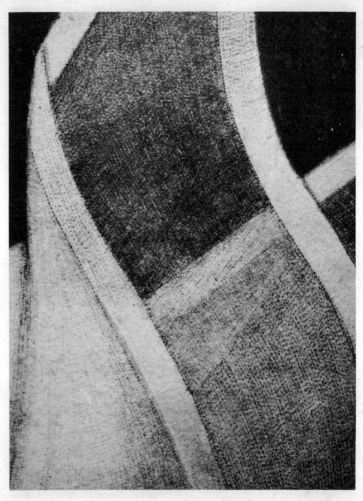

By running a rowel or spur over and over a plate its surface was covered with tiny pits and with corresponding spicules of metal that stood up from the surface in a burr like the pile of velvet. The lines followed by the spur in traveling over the plate can be easily seen in the accompanying reproduction. When the plate was inked and wiped the spicules held more or less ink depending upon their length, which in turn depended upon how much pressure was exerted upon the spur. The burr could be scraped or burnished down in places where it was too strong.

The invention of the rocker (see reproduction on page 8) later in the seventeenth century made it possible to lay an even, close burr all over the surface of the plate. The tints were then scraped or burnished into the even tone of the burr. Engravings printed from rocked surfaces that have been scraped and burnished down are known as mezzotints. This enlarged reproduction of the uncleaned edge of a mezzotint shows the effect of the rocker.

The most popular and rapid means of producing tints in the late eighteenth and early nineteenth centuries was by the etching process known as aquatint. In the usual eighteenth-century method rosin dissolved in spirits of wine was poured over a clean plate, which was then allowed to dry. In drying the rosin reticulated into little lumps leaving the plate bare between them. (Think of the way a mud flat dries into cakes in the sun.) The work then proceeded by an elaborate system of stopping out and biting (see page 60).

Mezzotinting is incapable of yielding really sharp edges or accents. It is therefore frequently pointed up by engraving or etching. In this early nineteenth-century example the artist etched the lines on his plate first and then rocked and scraped it. The final result in its natural size has somewhat the effect of a pen and wash drawing.

Aquatint, being incapable of sharp accents and thin lines, though only too capable of "hard edges," was frequently combined with line etching.

Stipple engraving was done by covering a plate with etching ground, making dots in the ground with a point, and then biting the plate with acid. It was a favorite eighteenth-century way of rapidly reproducing portraits and fancy heads in pencil and watercolor. It was often used in connection with roulette work (see pages 9 and 108).

The etchers and engravers of the eighteenth century not only learned how to make tones or tints but they learned how to make soft instead of hard lines. The etchers made soft lines by "soft ground" etching. They covered their plates with a mixture of ordinary etching ground and suet. Over this they stretched a piece of thin paper, on which they drew their picture with a pencil. This is part of such a pencil drawing.

Wherever the pencil touched the paper it pressed it down into the soft
ground so that in that place the ground stuck to the paper. When the
paper was peeled from the plate it took with it the ground that stuck to
it. The plate was then bitten with acid like an ordinary etching. This is
the part of the etching that corresponds to the pencil drawing on the
opposite page.

The engravers made soft lines by using roulettes, *i.e.,* tools with little wheels which had different sorts of spickers on their outer edges. As different treads on motor tires make different patterns in the dust so different roulettes made different marks on copper plates (see page 9).

Soft ground and aquatint were frequently used together in imitation of pencil and wash drawings.

On rare occasion an aquatint ground was bitten heavily and evenly all over a plate, or a portion of it, and was then scraped and burnished just as though it were a mezzotint ground. Little original work was done in aquatint, though some that was done was artistically of great importance. It was essentially an indirect method peculiarly suited for reproductive work.

At all times there has been fascination in very minute work. In England men engraved the Lord's Prayer on the head of a pin. In eighteenth-century France they made miniature portraits. The whole head in the original of this portrait is no wider than the iris of the eye in this enlargement. No one looking at the original with the naked eye can have any idea of the technical complexity of its workmanship.

COLOR IN PRINTS

The earliest use of color in prints is found in the earliest prints. The earliest single-sheet woodcuts and book illustrations most frequently occur daubed up with strong colors applied with a brush.

The earliest prints printed in color (*i.e.,* other than black or brown) were engravings. These, however, were not true color prints as they were monochromatic, only one color, red, green, or blue being used.

The earliest prints printed in several colors were woodcuts made by printing a line block and one or more flat color blocks on the same piece of paper. The line block was usually printed last. Pictorial woodcuts of this kind are generally referred to as chiaroscuros.

It was seemingly not until the late seventeenth century in Holland that anyone had the idea of inking an engraved or etched plate in different colors, such as blue for the sky, green for the foliage, and red for the tile roofs, and so forth. Impressions of this kind are said to be printed "à la poupée," poupée being the French name for the roll of paper or cloth with which the colors are rubbed into the different lines on the plate. Prints made in this way are always somewhat smeary or blurry, as it is not possible to make a sharp demarcation between any two colors. Plates in all the different techniques were printed à la poupée. In many instances the plates were printed in black or brown until they began to show wear, after which they were printed in color, thus rather effectively camouflaging the condition of the plate. In the eighteenth century engravers began to use a different plate for each color. Many prints printed in color received discreet retouching with water color. On rare occasions a combination of etched or engraved plates for the black lines and wood blocks for the color tints was used.

Probably more color prints were made in lithography than in any of the other techniques. A different stone was used for each color. Prints made in this way were called chromolithographs or, more familiarly, "chromos."

The commonest of all old colored prints are those that were painted up in water color after being printed in black or brown. Prints in black or brown ink that have been colored by hand have black or brown lines and the color lies on the surface of the paper between them. Prints printed in colored inks have colored lines and the paper between the lines is apt to be white.

As most of the peculiarities of color prints cannot be brought out in black and white only a few are here illustrated.

This is a portion of an Italian fifteenth-century woodcut book illustration colored with stencils.

This is a detail from a chiaroscuro. There are three color blocks and a black block. The color blocks were an afterthought and were a means of covering up the distasteful damages that had been sustained by an older block for a black and white woodcut. Some of the black lines in the left eye have been broken, as can be seen in this enlargement.

This is a detail from one of the most famous Italian sixteenth-century chiaroscuros. It can be seen that the black line block here serves merely to provide a series of accents in the flat tones of the other blocks (see page 112).

This is a detail from a technically simple sixteenth-century Italian combination of intaglio etching and relief tone blocks.

OF COPIES, FACSIMILES, AND OTHER
BOTHERSOME MATTERS

There are imitations and copies in all media, but there are really no such things as true facsimiles in any medium. The "facsimile," even when meant to deceive, is practically certain to betray itself, if for no other reason than that in these days it is all but invariably made by another process than that used in making the original.

In the following enlarged reproductions it can be seen how the lines in the originals are very different from those in even the best copies and facsimiles. A somewhat subtler difference is that introduced when an impression of a late state is doctored to look like an earlier state. A little discreet attention with a bit of sandpaper or a knife will often remove lines or dots, but luckily this cannot be done without making the paper suspiciously thinner in all too apposite a place. Worn, weak lines are helped by retouching with a brush and india ink. This happens very frequently in the boundary line (the "trait carré") that runs around the outside of a great many renaissance woodcuts. But again, luckily, india ink when thick enough to resemble the full line of the woodcut has a color different from that of printer's ink and is apt to have a little shine of another kind when seen in a raking light. Worn lines in an etching or engraving can be replaced or strengthened with india ink and a very fine brush, but a brush line when enlarged does not really look like an etched or engraved line. Discreet retouching of a mezzotint with a brush and india ink is also not unknown. The crossing of two lines printed from a plate or a block in the same pull of the press is composed of but one layer of ink. If the two lines are separately printed, or if one of them is printed and the other is drawn, their crossing, when greatly magnified, clearly shows two layers of ink. The crossing of two drawn lines is composed of two layers of pigment.

The retoucher, and the copyist who makes another block or plate, is most apt to give himself away because he has not understood the shorthand of the original artist, and sometimes because he tries to make things "too good." It is hard for the retoucher or copyist to realize that very often the maker of the original was not as clever as he is or was not possessed of the same technical means. A familiar example is a late impression with telltale marks of its lateness that has had its face remade in a beauty parlor—like the wrinkles of age, little scratches that come only with lateness are incompatible with too full lines in other places. A copyist or forger photographs an original woodcut on a block of end wood instead of a block of side wood, and then, instead of cutting the block with a knife, engraves it with an engraving tool, and out of anxiety to make as perfect a reproduction as possible betrays the fact that he has used a tool that the maker of the original could not have used. In photomechanical reproductions the accidental accompaniments of the printing of the original—the blobbet of ink on the side of a woodcut line, the smear of ink on the surface of the drypoint plate—are caught up and made permanent and unvarying parts of the printing surface. The original wood block presses the ink on the top of the line into the paper, while the blobbet of wet ink on its side is not pressed into the paper although it leaves its mark on it. In the reproduction both the top of the line and the blobbet on its side are pressed into the paper. The lines in a photogravure reproduction of an etching are shallow where the lines of the original plate are deep. The photogravure lines therefore do not stand up from the face of the print as do those of the original, and they cast none of the little shadows that are so important a part of the "quality of impression" of a fine original. It is a pity that most prints are only seen by artificial light because it is only possible to be keenly aware of these delicate qualitative things in raking daylight. In artificial light or top light they are extremely difficult to see. Because a photogravure is an etching it can never really have the character of an engraving, for the one is a shallow erosion and the other is a deep cutting.

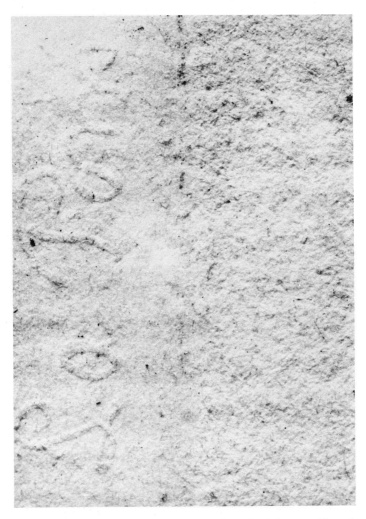

This is a detail from the margin of an etching by Meryon. After the printer had inked and wiped the plate but before he printed it, he wiped the ink out of the etched lines of the lettering on the margin. This made a late state look like an earlier state. The enlargement, however, shows the "blind" (*i.e.*, uninked) impression of the letters, which, standing up, however microscopically, from the surface of the paper, throw little shadows that can be read in a raking light.

This is a detail from a fine early impression of Marcantonio's engraving of the Death of Dido. On the opposite page is shown the same detail from a late impression from another plate of the same subject. Although Marcantonio's engraving has frequently been described, no mention appears to have been made of this other plate. Careful comparison reveals that while the outlines have the same measurements no two lines or dots are the same in the two prints.

Comparison of this detail with that on the opposite page betrays the fact that the lines in this are not as well drawn as those in the other and that they lack indicative quality. The lines in the other are purposeful gestures; the lines. in this are empty and without purpose. In their natural sizes these differences are not easily perceptible. Doubtless good early impressions from this plate masquerade as highly prized originals in many collections.

One of the most famous prints, as well as the smallest, made by Dürer was a little round Crucifixion engraved on a gold plate, which, after some impressions had been pulled from it, was mounted in the pommel of the Emperor's sword. It was not signed. There are three early versions and a number of later copies. For a long time opinion varied as to which of two of the early versions was the original. It is not easy to tell them apart with the naked eye.

In the eighteenth and early nineteenth centuries this version was considered the original. More recently, however, most students have claimed that the version on the opposite page is the original. There is obviously a limit of smallness below which even the most skilled engraver cannot retain his fully autographic quality of line.

In general the most deceptive copies made before the days of photography were those of woodcuts. In the early sixteenth century copies were made of woodcuts by the Master I.B. with the Bird which were so close that they were only recognized a few years ago. When enlarged, however, the difference is patent. In this original the lines have intention and meaning. In the copy on the opposite page the lines have lost their intention. They have all the characteristics of careless and unintelligent but laborious tracing. The forger probably pasted an original impression face down on his block, rubbed it thin, treated it with oil to make it transparent, and then cut his block through it—a process that was sometimes used when the drawing for a woodcut was made on paper instead of on the block. This forgery was reproduced by F. Lippmann as the original in his standard set of facsimiles, *The Woodcuts of the Master I.B. with the Bird* (Berlin, 1894).

In the middle nineteenth century, before photography was in general use, Pilinski of Paris was famous (and notorious) for the deceptiveness of his copies of old woodcuts. This is an enlargement from an original fifteenth-century Florentine woodcut. On the opposite page is Pilinski's wood-engraved copy.

Pilinski had to redraw his copy of the old and valuable original because he could not paste the original on his block and engrave through it. Every line is different—every line is stupid—and the whole character has changed. In a number of places Pilinski completely misunderstood the "indications" of the original.

After photography had reached the point where drawings and old prints could be photographed onto wood blocks, the copyist and forger of old prints frequently called the camera to his aid as a means of getting an accurate picture of his original onto his block. This is a detail from an original woodcut by Dürer.

This is the same detail that is shown on the opposite page as it appears in a wood-engraved copy made over a photographic base. The copyist not only misunderstood the lines in the original but made the crucial mistake of introducing white lines and flicks of a kind that can only be made with a graving tool and not with a knife. This forgery is particularly interesting because it was illustrated as the original in Scherer's *Albrecht Dürer*, in the well-known series of *Klassiker der Kunst*, in its 1904 edition, from which this reproduction has been made.

Facsimiles made before the day of photography were merely more or less careful handmade copies and actually had only a most superficial resemblance to their originals. The lines in most etchings are too fine to be traced off and have literally to be redrawn by the copyist. This is a detail from an etching on iron by the German sixteenth-century artist Jerome Hopfer

This is the best copy that an able etcher and copyist could make of the original on the opposite page. It was published at London in 1828 as a facsimile by W. Y. Ottley, the great collector and connoisseur of prints.

Facsimiles are made today by photomechanical methods. Some of these are deceptive at first sight, but enlargement tells the story. This is a great enlargement of a tiny head in the original of Schongauer's engraving of the Flight into Egypt.

This is a reproduction of a most excellent and carefully made intaglio photomechanical facsimile of the head on the opposite page, which was made from the identical impression there reproduced. It is taken from Max Lehrs's standard set of facsimiles of Schongauer's engravings published by the Graphische Gesellschaft of Berlin in 1907.

This is a detail from Legros's well-known drypoint Le Canal. The ink printed from the surface of the plate is smooth and unbroken except by the drypoint lines.

This is a process fake of the print on the opposite page—it was even
signed with a false pencil signature. What should be smooth unbroken
surface ink shows the broken grain of the photogravure process by which
the fake was made, and all of it lies below the surface of the clean-wiped
plate. Photogravure is a refined combination of photography and aquatint.

This enlargement shows how a restorer replaced a missing piece of a print by Mantegna with a different piece of paper on which he copied the missing engraved lines in pen and ink. This is a clumsy example chosen for its obviousness.

In the early nineteenth century a faker made up an Italian primitive
engraving out of whole cloth. It became famous as one of the finest early
prints and so before long another faker made a fake of it which passed
current as the "original." This enlargement of a small detail from the
second fake shows it up as an Italian print of the Romantic Period utterly
devoid of all fifteenth-century character.

This is a detail from a fairly honest impression of a Dutch primitive
engraving.

This is another impression of the same plate but one that "has had its face lifted" by a very able restorer, who has worked all over it with a brush in an ink somewhat paler than the ink of the printer.

This is a portion of an impression from an etched plate. It is therefore in reverse of the work on the plate, *i.e.,* what is the right hand on the plate is the left hand on the impression. A counterproof (see page 14) taken from an impression before its ink dries is in the same direction as the work on the plate. The lines in a counterproof are flat like those in a lithograph.

This is a "touched" counterproof (*i.e.,* one that has been drawn upon) of an early state of the print reproduced on the opposite page. The work on a plate is much more easily corrected or added to when the changes are worked out on a counterproof than on a direct impression, as they can then be carried over onto the plate without having to be reversed.

NOTES ON A FEW POINTS OF INTEREST

On the Social Importance of the Graphic Techniques

A print may be defined as an image made by a process that is capable of producing a number of exact duplicates. Such an image cannot be made directly by hand, for no copy is like the original from which it is copied, and no two copies are alike. This means that no two handmade pictures can tell the same things about the same object.

It can be reasonably argued that the great event of the fifteenth century was not the rediscovery of Greek or any other sort of ancient learning, but the discovery of mechanical ways to make pictorial records in duplicate, exactly, cheaply, and in vast quantities. This discovery made it possible for the first time to make pictorial statements and records in exact duplicate and to distribute them in invariant visual form simultaneously to many different people in many different places. The importance of this to human society can hardly be overstated. It has possibly had greater effects than any mechanical discovery since the invention of writing, as it is basic not only to our knowledge of the past and the present but to a very large number of our modern technological and scientific developments.

Since sometime in the 1400's men of the western European civilizations have derived from duplicate pictures most of their knowledge of the shapes and textures of things not immediately at hand.

Only the very smallest proportion of these duplicate pictures was made for specifically artistic as distinct from informative reasons. So-called fine prints are only an infinitesimal and indefinable portion of the total number of printed pictures. Fashions in collecting and the blindness of students of "art" to all things not baptized as "art" have led to an almost complete misunderstanding and even ignorance of the actual functions and developments of the duplicate picture.

Each generation has had its particular and favorite form of duplicate picture. First there were woodcuts, then engravings, then etchings, after which there came in order across the centuries, mezzotints, aquatints, wood engravings, and lithographs. Finally in the 1830's came the beginnings of photography, out of which in turn came the photomechanical processes which produce halftones, line blocks, and all the other modern means of illustrating books, magazines, and newspapers. With the exception of lithography each of the pre-photographic processes requires special techniques of draughtsmanship that are based upon the nature of its peculiar tools and materials. Lithography, having no specially shaped drawing tool, uses those of ordinary men, crayon or pencil, pen, and brush. Whatever tools and materials are used, only certain very restricted kinds of statements can be made with any combination.

Seeing the world through its duplicate pictures, each generation has unwittingly read the qualities and defects of its duplicate pictures into its knowledge of the world, just as the man who wears green glasses sees the world all green. The last great change in the conditioning of human vision happened when people began to see in terms of photographs. The recent development of color photography and its reproduction in printer's ink has already begun to have its marked effect upon the public's sense of color. (Compare the note on the Influence of Illustration on page 143 and that on Wood Engraving on page 44.)

In view of all this the importance of being able to recognize the technique or process by which a printed or otherwise precisely duplicable image was made becomes obvious—for this knowledge enables us to discount or make allowances for the limitations, the blind spots, the distortions, implicitly and unknowingly introduced by techniques and processes into duplicate images and their testimony about the world. These implicit distortions are a most important part of the unconscious, unphrased, common assumptions of any human society, which basically determine its ideas and action. Very few people ever realize the extent to which "objective facts" as known by us are actually no more than peculiarities of our instruments of observation and record.

From a purely artistic point of view, however, the recognition of graphic techniques has little reward for anyone who is not himself a practicing graphic technician. The fact that a particular print is in one or another process has no more bearing upon its artistic merit than has the fact that it was printed in the basement or on the top floor.

The Influence of the Illustration

One of the most important factors in the development of the printed picture has been the steadily growing use of illustrations in printed books. Very few illustrations are made for the purpose of expressing the illustrator's personality or as works of art. The great majority of them have come into existence as conveyors of information or as tools in the struggles of opinion. A very small proportion were made as decorations to printed texts. In the long run the illustrator has made his pictures not to suit himself but to serve the ends of his employers and the needs, real or fancied, of the community, in the elucidation of a text. Since 1500 the form of printed picture that the community has been most familiar with has been the illustration in its familiar books. Although single-sheet prints of the special kinds fancied by collectors of "fine prints" have almost always been executed in techniques or processes that were technologically obsolete, the greater number of single-sheet prints has at every time between the end of the fifteenth century and the end of the nineteenth century been executed in the techniques and linear styles that were for the moment most in use for illustration. The choice of the process and technique to be used in illustrating a book has, with few exceptions, always been dictated by a combination of economic and popular factors. Specifically artistic considerations have always played a subordinate role. Illustrations, like the books that contain them, have always been directed at particular social and intellectual groups, and the customs, pocketbooks, likes and dislikes of those groups have been as carefully as possible taken into consideration in the choice of the methods of illustration. The printed picture, like the printed book, has in the main been directed at the middle class rather than at the higher or lower classes and has conformed to its tastes and interests. The illustrated book has only flourished and been produced in large quantities in a bourgeois society. The engraved-plate books of the eighteenth century are only an apparent exception, as their method of illustration made their costs so high and their editions so small that only the wealthy could have them.

In general the principal function of illustration has been the conveyance of information. The graphic processes and techniques have grown and developed to the end of conveying information. The illustration that has contained the greatest amount of information, i.e., of detail, has been the one that was most in demand. As a result of this the graphic processes have shown an ever increasing fineness of texture. This increasing fineness of texture has repeatedly been carried to the point where the current process was no longer economically practicable, and then there has been a shift over to some other process that while producing approximately a similar result has been economically more advantageous. Thus the woodcut, which could be printed in one operation with the text, was for long the dominant mode of illustration. As time went on the texture of the woodcut got finer and finer until with the production of such cuts as those illustrated on pages 36 and 38 it became difficult, when not economically impossible, to print them in quantity on the papers and with the technical devices that were available.

The illustration on page 38 is dated 1557. After about that time the use

of engravings and etchings as illustrations became more and more common, and the woodcut began to be used less and less. After the early
1600's the woodcut retained its place as typical illustration only in the
volumes intended for the pedlar's pack and the country fair, *i.e.*, in books
for naïve and poor audiences. By the end of the following century the
texture of the copper plates in use for illustration had grown so fine that
the plates could no longer yield big editions, and illustration became
restricted to use in what may be called "de luxe" books. It is not without
its interest to note that none of the picture books in which the pictures
have become integral with the text in people's memories—*e.g.*, the *Shep-
herd's Calendar*, the *Epistole e Evangelii*, the *Life of the Virgin, Slovenly
Peter, Alice in Wonderland*—was illustrated with intaglio plates.

Just before 1800 Bewick in England and Senefelder in Germany invented wood engraving and lithography, both of which had textures
almost comparable in fineness to those of the copper plate and were at
the same time economically much more advantageous. For some years
the presses and inking methods were not competent to cope with wood
engravings of more than a few inches in area. The lithographic press,
however, could turn out large prints. The wood engraving rapidly took
its place in the texts of books, while the large full-page plates kept on
being printed from copper plates and, on the continent of Europe, began
to be printed from lithographic stones. As the nineteenth century wore
on, improvements in the presses and inking methods gradually made it
possible for wood engraving to be used in the making of full-page illustrations and eventually of the large double-page pictures in the popular
weeklies. But here again the demand for fineness of detail was insistent
and gradually led to a revolution not only in the techniques of the press
but in the manufacture of paper. The development can be easily traced
through the popular books and magazines. The illustrations in the *Century* of the early 1890's simply could not have been produced on the
paper and in the presses that produced *Harper's* during the Civil War.

By the beginning of this century the photomechanical relief processes
had come into general use and the older handmade printing surfaces rapidly lapsed from use except for very special purposes. Having thus lost
their general economic justification and stabilization most of the old techniques became languages used for their own sweet sakes rather than for
their power and utility. They left the work and the sweat of life and took
their places at the vicar's tea table, where their accents and manners were
of more account than what they thought and said.

The Important Techniques

It may in general be assumed that the greater an artist the simpler his prints are from a strictly technical point of view. This does not mean that they are necessarily easy to diagnose. Wood engravings (!) on end wood have been made with etching needles and even with sharp fragments of broken glass (A. B. Davies). Tints have been laid on etchings by scratching the grounded plates with sandpaper (Camille Pissarro). While wholly unorthodox, these methods are extremely simple. The more complex and artificial the technique of a print, especially in the way its lines are laid, the more certain one may be that its maker was a craftsman translator and not a creative artist. The price of virtuosity is abject slavery to a complaisant tool, that of creative artistry is willful dominance over a recalcitrant tool. The world has a curious but encouraging habit of forgetting the virtuosi. The only two techniques that really are of artistic importance are rarely or never mentioned in essays and books upon the graphic techniques. They are those of pictorial imagination and sharp-sighted, sensitive draughtsmanship. No one can ever be taught these two great techniques, for they are part of the eternal mystery of personality and its growth, to be recognized but not to be rationalized or reduced to a method. They can no more be imitated than wit.

Of Reproductive Prints

Until about sixty years ago most of the printed pictures that were made and collected were reproductions of paintings and drawings. In the late 1830's Fox Talbot, using paper negatives, made the first photographs. In the 1850's negatives on glass became practical. In 1879 George Eastman took out patents for the first machine to coat sheets of glass with a sensitive photographic emulsion. His patents for the first photographic films were taken out in 1884. The first halftone in a periodical has been said to be one that appeared in the New York *Daily Graphic* on March 4, 1880. The basic patent for the modern "crossline halftone screen" was issued in 1886. Today photography and photomechanical processes have taken the place of the classical handmade graphic techniques. Most of the change-over took place between 1880 and 1905. This has had great effect upon print making, both economically and artistically.

Of Reproductive Print Makers

The reproductive print makers, and they were at least ninety-nine percent of all print makers, were craftsmen copyists, or, as they preferred to be known, "translators," a euphemism that gave them much comfort. As the imagination, composition, and draughtsmanship were given to them in the paintings and drawings they copied, all they had to think about was their manual skill. Because the pictures reproduced were taken for granted, the questions to be asked about a print were not whether it was a good picture or drawing but whether from a technical point of view it was a good etching, engraving, and so forth, and whether from a comparative point of view it was a "fine impression." Today, thanks to photography, prints stand on their own feet as works of art and any need for knowledge or opinion about them as exercises in particular techniques has long since been submerged under the infinitely more important problems of their composition, imagination, and draughtsmanship. The answers to these problems require no knowledge of the reproductive techniques, and, no matter what the answers may be, they render any question whether a print is a "good etching" or a "good engraving" both pedantic and superfluous. Less than forty years ago Goya's prints were regarded as "bad etchings" and the masterly prints made by Daumier in the 1860's as "bad lithographs."

In 1653 Abraham Bosse wrote, "Pour celuy qui desire d'estre Graveur . . . tout le principal fonds qu'il doit faire est du dessein; car ensuite la Gravure, soit au burin ou à l'eau forte, ne luy sera qu'un jouet pour l'execution." A century and a half later William Blake summed the matter up when he wrote, "Painting is drawing on canvas, and engraving is drawing on copper, and nothing else, and he who pretends to be either painter or engraver without drawing is an impostor."

On the Economics of Print Publishing

It would seem that the first professional print publishers made their appearance in the first half of the sixteenth century. Publishers have rarely made their own prints and have usually hired other men to make them for them. They have not wanted prints by particular men so much as they have wanted prints of particular kinds representing particular kinds of subject matter. It is as economically easy as it is artistically regrettable to see why the print trade has always liked regular dependable producers of standardized goods, and has not favored contemporary print makers who have had adventurous developments and whose subject matters and techniques have showed much change or variety.

The growth of print publishing as a trade and a manufacture resulted in a separation into different professions of the practice of picture-making and the practice of the graphic techniques, so that at the École des Beaux Arts in Paris the painters and draughtsmen took one course and the print makers another. As in all similar situations this brought about not only a rather high average level of technical skill among the professional print makers but also rather a dead level of impersonal, undifferentiated skill. Engraving and etching became mechanical crafts. In the event the engraver all too often became a mere hand on an assembly line. From this shop practice developed the artificial linear structures and textures that for several hundred years were the outstanding characteristics of the commercial printed pictures that were made in such quantity. It has always been commercially desirable that engravings should be quickly made, for the engraver's time costs money and it is wasteful to tie up capital in idle plates. It was only possible to produce a series of engravings quickly by dividing the work among a number of different engravers. To preserve homogeneity in a series of engravings it was necessary that the engraving in all should be as nearly the same as possible. It was also desirable that several men should be able to work on the same plate according to their particular specialties. Therefore the engravers were taught and disciplined in conventional, artificial, linear systems. This reached perhaps its highest development of impersonality in the production of large white-line wood engravings for the weekly magazines, which were made on big blocks that came apart into little pieces, each of which was engraved by a different man. When put together again it was requisite that there should be as little difference as possible between the work on the several bits of wood in the big block. In time the engravers took pride in these goose steps and in elaborating them. The conventional linear systems became widespread—it is only the copybook hand that is easily imitated—and skill in them was looked upon as a test of an engraver's ability. It is very important, however, to remember that these lock-step linear systems were inherent, not in the technical processes with which they became associated in the popular mind, but in the economic setup of the highly organized manufacturing business that print making had become.

The so-called facsimile woodcut, in which the cutter's or engraver's task was to remove the wood from between the lines drawn by the artist on the block, was the only classical form of print manufacture which retained any of the original artist's lines. It is because of this that the illustrations in the woodcut books of the past are so frequently aesthetically superior to those in the copperplate books of the past. The illustrations in the old copperplate books, unless, as very rarely happened, they were engraved by the original designers, were merely copies, few good and many bad, of original designs in other media. This same thing was true of the wood engravings in white-line tints which were popular as illustrations in the second half of the nineteenth century. Lithography has a somewhat similar story. Although many great painters and draughtsmen have made original drawings on lithographic stones, not only as isolated works of art but as book illustrations, posters, political caricatures, and so forth, the overwhelming number of lithographs has consisted of mere routine copies in laborious techniques of designs conceived and first carried out in other media.

Of the Maintenance of Standards

On occasion one hears people remark that "artistic standards" should be "maintained." Less frequently one hears it said that "standards of quality" should be "maintained." Both remarks are based on a fallacy in reasoning that comes from an ambiguity in the meaning of the word standard. In manufacture and trade a standard is something that other things should and can exactly resemble. Standard dollars are interchangeable—it makes no difference which dollars one has, so long as one has a given number of them. The same thing is true of the standardized parts of a motor car and of standard quart cans of tomatoes of any particular brand. The great standard works of art, however, are the works of art that no other work of art is like. So far from being happy and satisfied when it is discovered that two works of art are just alike, people promptly become worried and unhappy over the situation. Experts are called in, lawsuits are started, and there is trouble until it is finally decided that they are not just alike and that one of them is a fake. The only standards that can be maintained are the very opposite of "artistic," because they are the standards of impersonalized routine production. If they were to be maintained in art, art would die. It is worth while to think how few of the reproductive and professional print makers of the past are remembered. They have been forgotten precisely because they standardized their quality and then maintained their standards. The man, like the society, which does this has stopped thinking and experiencing and become a mere machinery of frozen habit. Every new tool or material, every new process, and every change in religious or social theory and habit introduces change that is incompatible with "maintenance of standards."

Of Quality of Impression

"Quality," unfortunately, has nothing to do with the major artistic virtues such as imagination, composition, or draughtsmanship, but is a matter solely of the printer's skill and the condition of his printing surface. Whether or not a particular impression is a good or a fine impression is a matter only to be decided by direct comparison with other impressions of the same print or by memory of such other impressions. Only a very small number of people have dependable memories of this kind of thing, and no one has an infallible memory. If other impressions are not available then one has to take what he can get—and if anyone likes what he can get, it is a good impression for him. What is fine quality for one print has no bearing on what is fine quality for another by another artist. Any good artist has a quality of his own that is just as idiosyncratic as his drawing. When two artists have very nearly the same quality one or the other (and probably each!) is of very little artistic importance.

It is important to remember that as yet no one seems to know how the early engravers and etchers printed their plates, in what kind of a press, or under what pressure. The early impressions of early engravings, especially the large Italian ones, are often very irregularly printed, as though the plates had been very carelessly wiped after being inked in soft ink or oil paint that was carelessly rubbed into the lines, and as though the pressure in printing had not been the same all over the plate. While some lines have a lot of ink in them, others have little or none. The early impressions not infrequently seem to have slipped in passing through the press or its equivalent, so that some of the lines are smeared or doubled. There is reason to believe that the hard, even, late impressions of many of the early plates were printed long after the plates were made and by a press or other device of a kind not used in printing the early soft impressions.

There is rarely any need for having a modern print in poor condition. Fifteenth-century prints in fine condition are apt to be also rather late and poor impressions. Really fine early impressions of them are apt to be in rather poor condition. Almost the rarest things in the world are very old prints that are fine in both quality and condition.

Too great an emphasis on condition or quality of impression is apt to wind up by turning prints into precious stones or postage stamps instead of the drawings and pictures they actually are and removes them into some category quite other than that of works of imaginative art. It is said that according to modern fashionable standards many of the prints which

Dürer proudly gave to his great friend and patron the King of Denmark are mediocre impressions. A print which is only worth having in a very fine impression is doubtfully worth having in any impression whatever. The poorest impression of a really great print, no matter how shabby it is, is still a great work of art.

It is useful to remember that print makers, print collectors, and print users of the past never dreamed of us of today or of our tastes and prejudices in regard to quality and condition. The feeling that prints should not be colored, like the feeling that they are precious things to be kept in mats and handled as little as possible, is comparatively modern. Most of the very great old collections were pasted rather carelessly in scrapbooks, and big prints were kept loose in portfolios or drawers. Just as most primitive woodcuts were daubed up with crude color, so early Italian engravings and etchings were frequently either colored or heightened in effect by more or less discreet use of pen or brush. For a long time prints were regarded simply as pictures of which there were many duplicates (much as photographs are today), and not as things of a special kind with special values and special rituals. They were bought by artists and craftsmen for use and were part of the customary working equipment of the studio or shop. On occasion they were pricked all over or squared off as the easiest way of taking off their designs for use.

Of States and Watermarks

The beginner should make most careful differentiation between state, condition, and quality. They are quite different and in many instances are independent variables. Every change in the work on a printing surface as shown by comparison of the prints pulled from it indicates a change in state. These changes are sometimes made by the artist in furtherance of his pictorial idea, sometimes they amount to no more than a change in the punctuation of the name or the address of the publisher or dealer, sometimes they are made by any skilled hand that is available to cover up or disguise the wear that is inevitably undergone by the printing surface in the course of its use. Mere wear, by itself, however, even though it result in the complete disappearance of lines and the altering of values, does not make a difference in state. Condition has no relationship to either state or quality, but is a matter solely of the physical condition of the piece of paper on which the print was printed. Prints frequently occur that are late in state and horrid in quality but in superb condition.

At the very beginning of his study of prints the student is faced by one of the basic problems in that branch of philosophy known as epistemology. Most of the vast accumulation of learning about states, watermarks, and so forth, arises from the understandable but fruitless attempt to find describable marks such that knowledge of them through second-hand verbal description will take the place of first-hand sensuous recognition of quality of impression. For many print collectors these marks play the role played by the wine label for the man who tells whether a wine is good or bad by reading in a book and not by tasting in a glass. It is important always to remember that the condition, state, or watermark of a print carries no guaranty of its being a good impression, let alone a fine one. Most of the talk about quality of impression goes back not to first-hand judgment but to memory of verbal representations made in view of sale—*i.e.,* "mere campaign talk," which should be recognized as such. It is worth noting how few statements about quality are to be found on receipted bills.

Of the Lighting of Prints

The full quality of a print can only be observed in a raking white light, preferably daylight, such as falls from an ordinary window on a table. The person examining a print should hold it so that in looking at it he faces across the light and not into it. This is the way in which the texture of the paper and the highlights and shadows on the face of a print make their strongest effect.

The lines in an intaglio print (*e.g.,* an engraving or etching) stand up above the surrounding surface, which itself is slightly concave in the narrow spaces between lines. As light plays across an intaglio print the concave surfaces between the lines catch the light in microscopic highlights on the sides away from the source of light and have microscopic shadows on the sides towards the source of light. The shadows can be seen in the reproduction of a blind impression on page 119, and the highlights can be clearly seen in the left arm in the reproduction on page 77.

The lines in a relief print are sunk into the paper, so that they lie below the surrounding surface, which itself is slightly convex in the spaces between the lines. As the light plays across a relief print the convex surfaces between the lines catch the light in microscopic highlights on the sides towards the source of light and have microscopic shadows on the sides away from the source of light (see the reproduction on page 22).

An idea of the way the lights and shadows work can be gained from observing the lights and shadows on a shallow white saucer as it stands on a table first face up and then bottom up.

A print that has been too much washed or cleaned and especially one that has been subjected to strong pressure while damp is apt to have lost the relief of its lines and spaces and with it the shadows and highlights above described. For this reason many connoisseurs prefer old prints that are somewhat dirty or that have slight stains, but which still retain their full relief and texture, to others that have been cleaned and pressed.

At one time it was customary among framers to paste prints down flat on pasteboard or to paste them down around their edges while damp so that in drying they would become taut and flat. These methods were even used by dealers in fine prints. Each method is one of the worst enemies of fine prints, though the latter is not so disastrous in its results as the former, which has utterly ruined countless numbers of wonderful things.

Of Enlargements

It is frequently said that certain kinds of prints do not enlarge well or lose their interest when enlarged. The illustrations in this book prove, on the contrary, that all kinds of prints enlarge well. What does not enlarge well is not any particular kind of print but the work of particular (and all too many) artists. The work of any artist who has a marked sense of form or texture enlarges well. If an artist has little sense of form or texture his work enlarges badly. Form and texture are not merely local or superficial matters but dominate the whole composition and get down into the minutest detail, and an artist who has an innate sense of them on any scale has it on all scales. A print that seems to fall apart when enlarged was never really together. Enlargement merely makes artistic poverty more obvious. It is also obvious, of course, that any print can be fully appreciated for its aesthetic values only when seen in a good original in its original size, *i.e.,* without either enlargement or diminution. Changes in scale of the kind brought about by enlargement, although essential for technical examination, introduce changes in our physiological ocular awareness of values and brilliances, and distort our psychological reactions in many subtle ways. No careful study of this very interesting and important subject seems to have been made.

A Philosophical Note

On the next page there are two diagrams: one composed of black squares separated by white lines, the other composed of two squares made up of parallel lines. The squares in the second are exactly alike except that in one the lines are perpendicular and in the other they are horizontal.

If any one of the crossings of the white lines in the first diagram is looked at for a moment it will appear white but the other crossings will have flickering gray cores. If a crossing is looked at intently for a few seconds it also will have a flickering gray core.

Any person who has an astigmatism—and perfect eyesight is exceedingly rare—will see the lines in one of the two squares in the second diagram as being darker than those in the other. If the book is turned so that the horizontal lines become perpendiculars and the perpendiculars become horizontals, the darker square will become the lighter one.

These two experiments in the way the human eye works help to explain some of the specific qualities peculiar to many prints in black and white. Incidentally they point to the reason that reproductions, either in black and white or in full color, are necessarily untruthful in their values and hues unless they are of the same size as the originals from which they are made, even though they may be printed in identically the same pigments. Before one is through with the questions raised by these diagrams he has to wrestle not only with problems in the physiology and mechanism of vision but with a number of the basic problems in philosophy, more especially in the field of epistemology. To anyone interested in knowing how he knows what he sees and the extent to which he can and should trust his eyes these diagrams provide the starting point for fascinating and most important experiment and thought.

Two unretouched photographs from the same unretouched negative. Never trust a photograph of a print too much.

TABLE OF ILLUSTRATIONS

Unless otherwise noted originals of the prints reproduced are in the Print Room of The Metropolitan Museum of Art.